Beneath the Veil

of

Time

Wiss Auguste

Sentinel
Creations Press

Cover image by Thomas Skirde from Pixabay
Stock images from Pixabay

Visit my website at www.wissauguste.com
Instagram: @w.auguste.writes

Printed in the United States of America

First Printing: Jun. 2019
Sentinel Creations Press
www.sentinelcreationspress.com

ISBN- 978-1-7326955-2-8

"I write not to escape my reality, but to create the reality that my heart desires."

— Wiss Auguste

"And if tomorrow by some miracle, your love for me fades into a nothing, these words of mine will remain true until time is no more: *I love you*"
  — Wiss Auguste

Content

My Muse

A Garden of Roses

With every tear she shed,
a flower grew by her feet—
When the aching finally stopped
she found herself standing
in a garden of roses

Winter Was Kind

On a dreary brumal evening,
I trudged down the desolated streets.
My eyes wandered in awe:
Winter had turned the greenery
into a withered sheet of leaves.
Over the town as a whole,
It laid a white coat of sticky slush

Winter had spread its flurries
over the street lights,
  turning my short walk home
  into a melancholic plight –
Winter even froze the stream
of my leaky heart

On that same evening,
I met my muse under a leafless tree;
she took my hand and kissed it softly.
My cold hand touched the warmth of her face
and soon after, our fingers interlaced.
It was then that I realized winter was kind to her.
Her beauty bloomed in the cold dark night,
as vivacious as the winter flower

Pearls of Rain

Her cold, trembling lips,
covered with pearls of rain
are until this day
the sweetest I have kissed—

She left me ensnared
in this unhealthy obsession
with the autumn rain.

Whenever the sky opens up,
My senses go awry.
I sit by my window
and stare into the gray mists.
As raindrops dance across my roof,
memories of her heavenly kisses
race through my mind

Incomplete

She was stars
on a bleak autumn sky

The tantalizing scent
of thorny roses

Sweet honey stirred
in my Caribbean rum—

She was the good
that made my bad
bearable

Peace

She stepped into the light
and my once-frantic heart
found a steady rhythm;
There was something
bewitchingly soothing about her –
Maybe it was the Persian rose
tucked behind her ear,
maybe it was the magic
that lived in her eyes,
or maybe it was the mystery
in her serene gaze

Of Patience and Growth

Her demons twined around her
like vines on oak trees,
almost as if they wanted to stifle
every ounce of air out of her lungs

                    She silenced her roaring fears

                    and made time her ally

She flirted with her demons,
she teased them,
she tamed them,
she eased them into submission

Strength from Within

His love was everything to her.
She lived for moments
spent in his arms.
She enjoyed drowning herself
in the depth of his light hazel eyes.
He made her feel like time had stopped;
he made her feel as if she could float
 on clouds of endless love

"your kisses give me wings,"
she would often say to him

Yet, when he stopped loving her,
She soared higher than she ever thought she could.
Winds of her inner strength snuck under her wings
and carried her above the hurt

She was born to fly;
he weighed her down

Winter Flower

She loved him
like she always dreamt
of being loved;
the kind of love
that easily blossomed
through the harshest weather—
Yet, at the dawn of Winter
her love had withered,
strangled by his indifference

Just Once

There was so much hope
tucked beneath her skepticism—

All she needed was
to be proved wrong,
at least once

Forgiveness

She had forgiven him long ago.
Forgiving him had never been
what she struggled with

It is herself that she could not forgive.
Guilt was her eternal burden:
Things should have never gotten that bad
She should have never waited that long

A Gorgeous Mess

Her heart was a series of shattered pieces
that I tried to put back together—
My hesitant hands trembled.
I fumbled pieces of her,
like a child struggling with a puzzle

She grabbed my hand and smiled

"You can't fix it, darling,
just learn to love my mess,"
she said in the softest of voices

Midnight Talks

We moon-gazed until midnight,
we counted stars
and gave shapes
to all the shy clouds

I daydreamed of sensuous things,
things we could have done
if the night was a little darker,
and the wind, a little colder

She talked of magnificent things,
things she would have accomplished
If the world was a little kinder
time, a little slower
and men, a little wiser

Inner Joy

She'd always found so much joy
in watching other people
smile,
laugh,
and live

She'd always drew her peace
from the well of happiness
that other people bathed in

Yet, when she was all alone
in the dark of her mind,
she would shed sorrowful tears
until she could no more

One day, bright and new,
she gathered all the strength
stored within her core
and unburdened herself
of the weight of others

For the very first time,
her heart smiled from within

The Price of Closure

It saddened her to know
that he would eventually become
the man she'd always wanted
but the closure she seeks,
he could never provide –

It saddened her to know
that he would someday become
a better man, a caring man
but in her eyes, he will always be the man
who left her to wander
the dark alleys of self-doubt.

He will always be the man
who left her to rot
in a bottomless pit of depression

Marvelous

"You look marvelous,"
I whispered to her under my breath

"Aren't you a poet?
If I truly look marvelous
Write a poem about me," she joked.
Her words left me perplexed

Yes, I am a poet.
Yes, she was a marvel,
but no poet on earth
could describe something
that transcends all senses

Twilight in a Jar

There was a young demoiselle
who lived in the house up the hill.
She had magic in her eyes;
she was art,
she was a dove,
she was my dearest wish

Every day she promenaded
by her little garden
with a rose behind her ear.
She weeded the flower bed for hours,
as she hummed romantic tunes

She never talked.
Some say she was a sad angel
who fell from the heavens.
Some say she was dangerous,
dark,
mysterious.

I never cared who she was
nor what she was.
Angel or demon?
I longed to love
her joys and tears

My affection, of course,
as intense as precocial,
only lived within my soul.
To her, I was a mystery,
a stranger,
a wanderer

I, the wordsmith,
proud and bold,
opted to declare my flame
through a vivid poetic scheme.
I wrote a poem, long and sweet
about the sway in her hips

The following morning,
I woke up before the rooster's tune.
I walked to the house up the hill
to hand her my sweet idyll.
Yet, I froze as she walked past me:

her hair danced in the wind;
her hips were in cadence.
She had grace in her steps
and a whiff of chamomile
embedded in her shadow

I quickly understood
the weakness of my words.
My unflattering rhymes,
although carefully thought,
were an insult to her beauty.

Shameful,
inadequate,
I shredded my poem to pieces
and set my feet on a journey
to make up for my slight

I traveled through
raucous mountains
in quest of something holly,
something that would compare,
even slightly,
to her smile and her glee

hopeless, tired yet able,
I ventured beyond the wet plains.
Days and nights,
soaked in sweat but drenched in love,
I traveled through the rainforest.

I crossed county lines
and tortured my spine
at all ungodly hours.
I defied ungodly powers
that haunts the dense vines
all the way to the tree lines

As I began to lose hope,
I looked up in the horizon
and I saw the tired sun,
once glorious and bright,
succumb to its inevitable fate

The sun sadly stumbled
over cascading clouds
and slipped
behind the mountain's peak.
Quickly, quickly!
I hurried my steps!

I climbed the northern face
of the taunting Mount Elsemore
and I reached over the horizon.
Before the last ray of sunshine
disappeared into oblivion,
I caught the twilight in a jar.

With the same haste in my step,
I slid on my buttocks
down the mountain's slope
and rushed back to her divine demure.
I placed the jar sideways
on her front porch
with a message that read:

*"Please forgive the meager appearance
of this laughable jar.
I'd hoped to find you something
that remotely matched your beauty.
I know this twilight is still no match,
but it is the best I could do."*

Rebel

I saw a spark of defiance
scintillating
in the depths
of her eyes—
I immediately knew
she did not need saving,
She just wanted to rest
in the cradle of my chest

Vulnerable

I built a fortress around
my weaknesses and fears,
I draped this blanket
of solitude over my heart;
Oh, what an arrogant fool I was
to think I had defied love—
She smiled once
and became my world

Self-Destruction

Days after days,
she patched him up
with pieces of herself—
So, when he became whole
she became obsolete

There's an Angel in my Bed (Unworthy)

I could always find ways
to convince her,
or myself,
that we were meant for each other.

I could always find words
that matched our story
and moments that fitted us like gloves.

I could always draw anecdotes
from our misplaced kisses
just to prove to her,
or to myself,
that we were nature's answer
to the plight of loneliness

Yet, in the early mornings,
I would wake up,
and she would still be asleep.
I would gaze at her cheeks
gracefully resting on my pillow.

I would timidly touch the contour of her lips
not just because they were perfect,
but because I needed to know
that I wasn't merely lost in her dream.

An angel sleeps in my bed every night.
And every morning,
I am reminded that I am unworthy—
Unworthy of her presence,
unworthy of the love she pours into me
 from her ever-flowing fountain

The Riddle in her Eyes

She wears a veil of mystery
that intrigues
and frightens—
If only I could solve
the riddles in her eyes!

Unequivocally Unique

Everyone kept telling her
how different she was.
she could sense pity
in their patronizing voices:
insults dressed as compliments

So, she closed her eyes
to stop the noise—
deep inside she knew
She was much more
than just different;
she was
unequivocally unique

Her Smile

On days that the sun does not shine
and rainclouds shroud my sky,
her smile alone brightens my life

Untamable

Her inner demons
were never meant
to be conquered;
They were meant
to be set free—
There was
a wealth of beauty
amidst her chaos

Ode to my Muse

My muse,
My weakness
My strength—
Why have you forsaken me?
Why have you condemned me
to sit idly by and languish
in this perilous drought of words?

Dancing in the Dark

Dusk draped the day
for a while
before total darkness
descended on the dance floor

        A delightful demoiselle
        dashed out of the dark

She dazzled
in her little red dress
and defiantly danced
to the sound of drums

Despite my dubious delusion,
I made a drastic decision
to dive
into her den of delirium

And I, once dauntless
and daring,
stood in her presence
as docile as a dove

Hurdles

Behind every successful woman
is an unwavering determination
to get over hurdles
that touch the roof of the sky

Her Silence

I fear very few things in life;
I fear failure and death.
I fear failure
more than I fear death—
But her silence tops
my list of phobias

Take me With You

"Take me with you," she said.

"Darling, I cannot.
Where I am going, there are unkind souls
that will happily prey on the innocence in your eyes.
There are summers so hot that the scorching sun
will burn through your delicateness.
There are winters oh so cold—
And people with hearts colder
than the coldest of winters.
Sorry, darling. I cannot take you with me,"
I said to her.

"Ok. I understand. Now, take me with you,"
 she said once more.

Side by side, we journeyed through life.

Carefree

I knew not
what freedom
truly looked like
until I saw her
dancing in the rain—
Light on her feet,
her arms spread open,
her hair a happy mess

Magical

She had this uncanny ability
of knowing exactly
when my mind was under siege

Her soft hands
would caress
the back of my head—
Soothing, gentle strokes
that silently screamed
"It's going to be all right"

Her

Some days she was serenity—
The sweetest of voices,
the softest of touches,
kisses as gentle as
the first light of dawn

Some days she was a raging gale;
She had a storm
brewing at her very core—
A wrath of frustration
ready to be unleashed on this treacherous world

Yet, even on her darkest day,
she was still my bright lodestar.
She was wildfire, I was wind.
Together we knew we would win

Serenity

I looked up
and there she was...
She stood over me majestically,
spreading her vibrant wings of hope

'She looks like the peace I seek'
I thought to myself,

Serenity (2)

Battered by the vicissitudes of life
I walked home
defeated and frightened

My muse,
awaiting by the door,
took me in her arms
and rested my head on her shoulder –

As her fingers wandered
through my kinked beard,
the world stopped turning,
my heart stopped racing
and my frown dissipated
to make room for a smile

A Blanket of Stars

I wrapped my muse
in a blanket of stars,
hoping to hide her scars.
Yet, my ill-advised ruse
upset her very much...
"Why did you decide
to behave as such?
Was it to protect my pride?
Darling, are you not aware
that all the scars I bear,
just like the unique ametrine*
under the sun, shine?"

Ametrine: Gemstone only found in the Anahi mine in
Bolivia. No two Ametrine cuts look alike; the color
combination varies in every single cut. The gemstone itself is a
natural combination of two gemstones, amethyst and citrine.

A Letter to my Ex

'I woke up this morning
with tears on my cheeks,
meshed with remnants of the smile
you left there yesterday.
I am aware
that you no longer care
but are you aware
that you've left me in despair?
Knowing the coldness in your heart,
I should not even be writing to you.
What else could I expect from you
besides this selfish neglect?

I wish you the best,
but I want you to know that
goodbyes are always hard
but they are always better
than not a word at all.'

Her Voice

Having not traveled to the heavens,
I don't know for certain
what angels sound like –
But there is something divine
in the way she talks

The Intricacies of Love

Things Left Unsaid

Of all the things
left unsaid,
I love you
haunts me the most

Insanity

I suppose one could say
I should have known better—
Then again, maybe I did know better.
Maybe I knew that at the end of it all
I would be left with a broken trust

Maybe I knew better all along
but I still chose to love you,
not because I was naïve
but because I knew
moments spent by your side
would become my most cherished memories

Prisoners of Our Past

I wish you didn't have
to act so cold
to protect your heart—
I wish I didn't have
to try so hard
to prove my love.

Yet, things being what they are,
I will climb
the walls of your fortress
even it takes me a lifetime

Boomerang

How many times will we have
to go down that same road?
How many times can we say *goodbye*
until we really mean it?
How many *I am sorry* is too many?
How many different ways can you kiss me
before I accept that your lips are poisonous?
How many gulps of your poison
will I have to swallow until this doomed love dies?

Belonging

I would gladly brave the hellish flames
by your side If the heavens refuse
to grant both of us passage
through the Pearly Gates.

Whether it be Heaven or Hell,
where you are is where I belong.

Full Moon

Some nights, when I try to escape my mind,
I lost myself into the starless sky
until my tired eyes slumber—
And some nights,
when the gods want to punish me,
they reveal the moon to my undeserving eyes

They know that whether
the moon was round and grandiose,
or just a luminous crescent,
I could always see you in it

They know that, just as I did the moon,
I only loved you when you were full,
too shallow to appreciate
the beauty in your gloom

Puzzles

My biggest regret in life
is that I had to share my love
with more than one person —
Bits and pieces of my broken soul
are now scattered around.
I have secrets,
with keepers I don't remember.
I left fragments of my love
in places I shall never revisit.
I have a few *I love yous* that are
forever lost in the midst of yesterday.

The Innocence of Youth

The pain of watching another man
love the woman I was meant to love
is the ultimate punishment for mistakes
I dared blame on the innocence of youth—
If only I could go back in time
I would teach my young, impetuous self
to love her in ways that only gods can

Cultural Conundrum

She called it a cultural conundrum—
She said I could never understand
the way she was taught to love.

And I remember saying to her
that whether it be here,
or there,
whether it be across the dead sea
or below the western hemisphere,
Love conquers all hearts in a similar fashion.

Is it not true that all hearts flutter
when love enters?

Is it not true that,
whether we are from here or from there,
yellow, black, white or red,
Love conquers our heart
equally unpredictably?

Lost at Sea

I engraved my ineffable truth
in the sand of life.
I watched waves of unforeseen
misery crash onto my shore
and wash away my thoughts—
Now my secrets are lost at sea,
up for anyone to find,
up for anyone to see

Old Sentiments

I have an old, decrepit drawer
filled with unfinished poems—
And they will stay that way
until the end of time
because I refuse
to relive losing you

Love Me, Love Me Not

I never really know
what to expect with love.
Some days, it's the most beautiful thing
like a stardust-sprinkled rainbow
dancing under the drizzles.
And some days,
It's just a splintering word
that crawls under my skin
and rummages through my flesh –
Some days, I crave it
and some days, I run from it
as if it was the plague

The Inbetweeners

They were caught living an alternate truth:
prisoners of their age,
misunderstood,
prematurely birthing kisses and tears

Their head was filled with teenage dreams,
Their heart, filled with a semblance of love

Their *yeses* occasionally meant no—
They relied on each other
as a clock would rely
on a broken pendulum.

Young love, they called it:
a sad succession
of misguided decisions
that they made in tandem

Blame it on Me

I could have loved you
like you really wanted
to be loved
but life had other plans
for my heart,
and yours—
Now he is hurting you,
and I am hurting myself,
thinking of you every night

Unsteady Rainbows

She dared me to prove
that I truly loved her
So, I tiptoed on the arch
of unsteady rainbows,
looking for heavenly flowers—
I brought her
a bouquet of roses
blessed by angel's tears

My Forever

There will come a day
when my legs will wobble
and my voice will quaver;
The hair on my head
will become a distant memory
and wrinkles will map my journey on my skin

When that day comes,
I want to look to my left
and see you by my side.
I want to hold your hand
and travel east into the Great Unknown.
I want my forever to end
with you standing over me,
holding my hand,
as the last breath of life escapes my body.

The Curse of Jealous Gods

I once read in a book
written for princes and kings
that true, undying love
was nothing but a curse
from angry, jealous gods

And from that day on,
I have searched the world
for infinite ways
to anger jealous gods

Anchored

My happiness is anchored
to her smile—
When she frowns
I cry inside;
If I ever see her cry,
I fear I might die inside

Reciprocity

I fear the love I have to give;
I fear the passion
burning within my core

I fear these heartbeats
pounding the walls of my chest
when you are around

Can you ever love me
as much as I love you?

Silent Words

When silence befell us,
we talked in glances and smiles—

No words were ever needed;
she understood the language of my soul

My Ego, My Foe

She walked away...

I wanted to grab her hand...
A burning desire to apologize
overtook my senses—

"Love is overrated,"
whispered my ego
in my susceptible ears

So, I stood there
and watched her walk away
to never come back

The Curse of a Midsummer Kiss

And fireflies flooded the foggy air,
a faint glimmer of almost-hope
a spark,
a star that fizzled away
before it was allowed to shine

What was time
to timeless moments?
What was tomorrow
to two souls lost in the firmament?

Evermore, I savor bitterness on my lips
left to linger by her poisonous kiss.
Evermore, I long for sweeter lips
to efface these haunting memories

I Chose You

And if one day I am ever asked,
why I chose you
when I could have had
anyone I wanted

I will tell them the unequivocal truth:

'I chose her because she isn't
like anyone else
and because there's no one else I want'

Sweet Lies

Nothing warms up the heart quicker
than the comforting sound
of the lies we don't see coming

I do not blame you
for stomping on my heart,
I blame it all on my predisposition
to believe your twisted tongue

The Poem

To her, my words
were fictional
and my pain,
imaginary—
She saw a beautiful mind,
a wordsmith,
a musician

But I was a troubled mind,
a bleeding heart,
a lost soul

She loved the poet
but I was the poem

Dangerously Passionate

All of me,
or none of me,
that is all I have to give—
And
in love,
as in hate,
my passion falters not

Love me Now

How cruel of you
to postpone my love —
Tomorrow is made
of hope and dreams
but today is as real
as this ray of sunshine
that gleams across your face
when you smile with such grace

Young and Bold

In the fold of midnight,
the heavens opened up
and tears of the dying moon
came crashing on us—
But we did not care,
we dared to live free,
we dared to love freely.
we were drenched to the skin
and we were oh so cold,
but we were young and bold

Of Love and Convenience

Love, of all sentiments,
does not thrive on convenience—
The only way to truly love
is to harvest a love so pure
that it becomes
the very air we breath

I Love You

I gazed at her
with passion in my eyes—
One hand gently grabbing
the back of her neck,
the other one rested
on her divine hips

I pulled her closer to me
she leaned in,
I placed a kiss
on her shivering lips;
She then looked up
with subtle guilt in her eyes

"I love you", she murmured.
These enchanting words
crawled into my mind
and found lodging within me—
She had hijacked my heart
in the most unsuspecting way

Tears of Shame

When I look in the mirror
I seldom recognize
my own reflection.
Tears of shame
vagabond on my cheeks—

How did I get there?
Where did I go wrong?
Have I loved you
so much that I forgot
to love myself?

Maddening Sentiment

I don't care how many times
my heart has been broken.

I don't care how many times
I have had to carry my soul
into the drunkard's paradise
and drown my pain in whiskey —

I will not settle for mediocre love!

If I am to ever love again,
I want it to be as intense as the first time:
Mad... Uncontrollable... Unexplainable

I want my heart to be at the mercy
of someone who equally yearns for such
maddening sentiment

Infidelity

There's no word
strong enough to express
the pain I feel within my soul
every time you lay
those sweet kisses on me
with your treacherous lips.

Deep inside, I know
I could never hate you
but I also know
I can no longer love you

Fragments

I used to be terrified of heartbreaks
until the subject of my deepest affection
shattered my heart

in
    pieces
        so
            small

that I had to sweep away
the fragments

Everything

She tried to feed the fire in his soul
with love that he could not return –
She would have done everything
to see him happy
but even her *everything*
would have not been enough;

> She tried to fill the void in his heart
> with joy that he could not afford—
> He clasped onto his pain
> As if it was a lifeline;
> he feared happiness
> more than he feared loneliness

A Glance

It could have been romance
or it could have been lust
but we will never know –
All we shared was a glance.

Now I am left with half-a-memory
of a love I never had

Incompatible

I loved the idea of us.
I loved the idea of us holding hands
and walking down
the busy streets of New York City—
Yet, our demons refused
to play along;
Our egos, selfish by nature,
refused to cohabit

Selfish Love

Is it selfish of me to find satisfaction
in knowing that someone else had loved her
so wrong for so long?

I often ask myself:
Would she have ever appreciated my love
if she had never known
what it's like to love and not be loved?

Undone

Once my fear of losing you
slowly began to overshadow
my desire for your soft embrace,
I knew it was time to let go

No Greater Poem

The day she kissed my lips
was the day I understood
that a poet's greatest curse
was to experience emotions
that words could not quite describe

It was also the day I understood
that there is no greater poem
than the one never written –
No greater poem than the one
that lives within us
and pulsates through our veins

Rainfalls

Crystal clear drops of water
falling from the sky;
crystal clear drops of anger
falling from my eyes.

When it gets so dark outside,
lovers and hookers collide,

Wet trees and roofs, hazardous roads,
slippery sidewalks and adulterous toads,

Wet pillows,
witnessing heartbreak and distress;
Hurtful thoughts:
My lover is someone's mistress

Ten Thousand Flames

Love me with the passion
of ten thousand flames
and if one ever dies out
let's replace it with ten—
I want the kind of love
that makes me fall in love
a little more at every new dawn.

I want my doubts and fears
dissolved into nothingness
at the mere sight of you;
And I want your soft lips
to erase the memories
of all kisses before you

The Myth of Certainty

My father once told me
'Son, There's no certainty in life.'
And I believed him.
Then I became my own man
and I became certain
that the water that quenches my thirst
can also drown me;
The fire that keeps me warm
can easily scorch my skin
and your love, which keeps me whole
will eventually break me

Fleeting

Go on!
Go on, darling!
Follow your dreams—
The gentle scent
of Damask rose
embedded into my pillow
will keep sweet memories alive
until we meet again

Symbiosis

Our love was unlike any other love.
It was neither seen nor heard,
but always felt, oh so intensely,
Always deep-rooted in our souls!

A series of symbioses,
A series of unspoken words
that told a story—
A story that only made sense to us.

Here's to Never Again

To the half-smile we've shared
with a lover,

To every overlooked mistake
that dragged us unforgivingly
into a rabbit hole of recycled sentiments

                              To the tears we've shed
                                    for a lover,

                        To every silent scream
                        muffled in our entrails
                          as we seethe at night

To the lies we've heard
from a lover,

To every twisted excuse
that left us entangled in our thoughts,
trapped in a maze of deceit

Trust Issues

I believe trust issues to be
like fireflies in the night.
They can hardly be missed,
scattered over an open field.

Yet, once the moonlight spreads
across this field of flies,
they all vanish into oblivion,
as if they were never there—

Darling, would you be my moonlight
and spread across my field of flies?
because my heart craves a peace
that my mind won't let me have

A Dance with the Gods

I often gaze into
the darkness of the sky,
hoping to see your face
once more!
And when the moon
shines its light
over these somber clouds
I can almost see you,
dancing with gods and angels

In memory of my father, Joseph Vicent Auguste

What is Love?

'What is love?'
You asked.
I do not know.
I do not know what love is
but that doesn't mean I am lying
when I say I love you.
I do know that
the universe is only whole
because you are beside me;
My heart only beats
because you exist—
When you leave my side
I become a lost soul

Unconditional Love

Unconditional love is only that
of a mother to her child—
If I ever pour my all into you,
please fill my void with your trust.
Hold my hand as I hold yours,
kiss my lips as I kiss yours;
let the beating of our hearts
set the rhythm to our love!

Boundaries

And just like any human being
who has been, in one way or another,
slighted, played or used,
I understand the importance of boundaries —
Yet still,
I fell for the false sense of comfort
that you innocent voice provided

My Torturous Friend

She offered me friendship
just like one would offer a gun
to a suicidal man—
She knew there was
no greater torture on earth
than to talk to her every day
and not be able to kiss on her lips

Of Hugs and Heartbeats

I pulled her against my chest
and she rested her head on my shoulder
"I enjoy your hugs very much," she said.

Little did she know that
when I pulled her close to my racy heart
I simply wanted her to feel
the fear of dreadful lonesomeness
escaping my body

Notes to Self

Guard your wounded heart fiercely.
Once you see your walls disappear
Like seemingly sturdy sandcastles
Dismantled by unforeseen waves,
Accept that you've found love

The Social Construct

The Myth of Tomorrow

But what if tomorrow
never comes?
What if your *forever*
ends before nightfall?

If your sun sets tonight
to never rise again
would you be satisfied
with the life you have lived?

Worth the Risk

I cannot help but cringe
whenever I hear someone say,
I am worth the risk —
Why would you ever
think of yourself
as a risky endeavor?

The Gift of Dawn

I have found dawn to be
the most beautiful
yet, the most treacherous
gift of nature.

As the light of hope breaks
through heavy clouds
and illuminates the sky,
creatures of the night
still lurk in the almost-dark—

So, here I stand,
at the dawn of my life
shedding the burdens
of my nightly fiends,
welcoming the light
of new beginnings.

Here I stand,
terrified that creatures of the night,
emboldened by my fear,
might creep back out
and overwhelm my mind

Beneath the Veil of Time

As I hid beneath the veil of time
I saw flying by,
my good years and my bad—
Happiness came and left,
tainted at times by bouts of sadness

I longed for days better than yesterday
I longed for tomorrows better than today
and I waited,
and I waited,

I waited for infinite joy,
but it never came.
I waited for bottomless doom,
but it never came.

It was there,
hidden beneath the veil of time,
that I learned a valuable lesson:

In life, joy and pain interlace
and feed off each other.

Strength from Within

Those who claim that their words
hold the key to your freedom
also intrinsically imply
that their words can bound you in shackles

You do not need my words
to set you free—
You were born free,
you were born with the strength
that you have spent years
denying yourself

Onward, Always (The Myth of Stillness)

I believed myself to be trapped
in the stillness of monotony—
Everything around me stopped moving:
My growth, stunted by fear,
my dreams, cut short by rude awakenings
and my life, as stagnant as still water
with the occasional ripples

I believed myself to be trapped
in the stillness of monotony—
But the old clock on my wall
never stops ticking.
The hourglass of my life,
already half-empty,
leaks a steady flow of time
that I can never get back.

Not There Yet

The poet laughs and banters,
he always seems so joyful,
always so lively—
But he still has poems
that he can't share just yet.
He still has nightmares
that he can't shake just yet.
He still has memories that linger,
and heart wounds that fester.

The Social Contract

While we lie there, unaware,
with our back curved
and our head bowed
curled up, vulnerable, bare
within the snug wombs
of the women to whom we owe life

The whole world works restlessly
at molding our moral compasses—
A list of chastisement for our trespasses:
"Girl, this is beautiful, and that's ugly!"
"This is right and that is wrong!"
"Boy, don't you dare cry! be strong!"

If only we were allowed a say
on norms that, over us, hold so much sway

Of Lust and Longing

When hope escapes us
and the truth betrays us

When we find ourselves
trapped between
the hinges of solitude
and the uncertainties
of tomorrow

We latch onto this
illusory happiness
and allow ourselves
to be fooled by
the butterflies in
our guts

Happiness

On my ill-fated quest
for this ever-elusive perfection,
I overlooked happiness.

My American Dream

I grew up being fascinated by America
My American dream was made
of sunflowers and autumn breeze
that carries the scent of lilies
to my nostrils in the early morning

I'll tell you, I am now living that dream
and it is, in fact, not a dream at all—
It is an unending nightmare

It is misogyny laced with indifference,
it is racism laced with hypocrisy
it is backstabbing schemes
with a pinch of kindness

It's a poisonous concoction
of bigotry, greed and sexism
that I am forced to sip from—
And every day, something dies in me

Simpler Times

If only I could hop
on the wings of destiny
and soar back to simpler times—
To a time where love was truly free

The Birth of Activism

I thought I could tiptoe
my way, unscathed
through the broken pieces
of human's bigotry and ignorance—

I know now that I was
utterly delusional.

Now my words bleed resistance
and my heart longs for a change
that will rip through the very core
of the status quo

Breaking Free

Let's escape
through the rainforest—
Let's sit by a waterfall
and listen to its singing streams

Let's break those
self-imposed chains
and run free,
and run wild.

Let's run
from dawn to dusk
until we reach
the edge of our horizon

Only then can we look back
and be proud of the life we've lived

The Lenses of Perception

Is it not amazing
how the human mind works?
The way we perceive things
dictates how we handle them—
What you called shrubs
I call wildflowers.
So, when you ripped her off the ground.
I replanted her seeds.
I watched her bloom freely,
and wildly,
as nature intended

Why do we Roar?

Why do we roar?
Why do we resist?
Why do we defy the odds
and challenge the status quo?

It is because we can,
but more importantly,
it is because we have a duty
to be human above all else

At the Crossroads

I find myself
caught up
in this eternal
tug of war
between reason
and emotions—
My heart is likely
to be the only casualty

The Future of Our Past

This one is for the unforeseeable things,
for the intricacy of fate,
empty theories of doomsday
wrapped in a cryptic fear of the afterlife

It is for the mysteries
of unspoken tomorrows,
for good fortunes
and misfortunes

It is for the savory
fruits of hard work,
and the gullibility
of those condemned to fail

It is for all our mistakes,
the 'I should have known betters',
the memories that stay hidden
into the abyss of our subconscious,

For the embarrassment that swims up swiftly
    every time we listen to that one song,
    or that one verse,
    or that one voice

    This one is for the lives,
    lived as outcasts
    for the shame,
    carried like an overcast

    This one is for legacy:
    It is a look at ourselves
    through our fathers' eyes—
    A glimpse at a brighter future

    Or maybe,
    a look at ourselves in the void
    left by our fathers' demise—
    The grief we learn to nurture,

When the rest of us become dust,
all that is left to hold onto
is the unbearable vagueness
of memories that once were
joy,
or pain,
or both.

Black Man

I was taught to be a man…
A manly man…
A manly man does not cry
nor feel;

Then I was taught to be black,
the 'real' kind of black,
always slighted,
always a revolutionary —

But to be human,
that, I learned on my own.
As a human being,
I cry when my pain overflows
and I gladly allow joy
to replace the anger in my soul

And yes,
my revolutionary fire
burns in fiery flames
but I only let it roar
when I want to
not when I am told to

The Sins of Our Fathers

Yes,
we bathe in the sins
of those who came before us—
But is it not our duty
to break the cycle
once we have realized
the horror in our fathers' ways?

Gagged Mind

Hush now, beautiful mind!
Today is not the day
to buzz in my ears
like a bee in a box

Hush now!
I no longer want to hear
of your what-ifs,
and your maybes
and your cryptic fears

Hush now!
And let me spread my wings!
I will let the wind carry me
to all the places
you forbade me to go

A Pillow Named Melancholia

I know not
what the future holds
but when I close my eyes
at night,
I squeeze my pillow
as tightly as I can
and I wish for all the joys
that fate stole from me.

Carpe Diem

You are not half-alive—
Why should you live half-a-life?

Introspection

To keep a small circle of friends
is a true sign of wholesomeness
until that circle
becomes your prison
and their opinions
become your shackles

Repressed Memories

We all have

                                                        pain

that hides where joy
could never reach

Opportunistic Behaviors

Always be mindful of those
who build their home
on the ledge of your life
as they await better odds

Commitment
is not a game of card;

The Battle from Within

At the midpoint of nonsensicalness,
where greed meets confusion,
where romance meets deception,
there is a raging battle
between sheer wit and brute force –
There is a conflicted soul
seeking a balance where there's none

Not a Thing

Sometimes,
the best feeling
in the world is to not feel a thing—
But if you linger
in that emotional drought,
you will slowly sink
into an abyss
of dreadful loneliness

True Happiness

Now let me ask you this,
do you really believe
in the depth of your soul
that you can cheat your way
through happiness?
Who Is it that you aim to impress
with your unimpressive tales?
Who is it that you aim to fool
if not yourself?
Do you not know that
true happiness comes from within
and reflects on your skin
like oil on water?

Fleeting Moments

She welcomed me into her home.
Everything was so well-kept,
so meticulously placed,
so spotless
  Except, the dusty clock on the wall.

"That is one odd clock you have got there,"
 I said to her.

"Odd and broken," she replied.

"Then why not get it fixed?" I asked.

"Because I do not need to be reminded of the time.
 I already know all there's to know about time.
It is but a series of fleeting moments,
Just ephemeral joys we try to catch in passing," she said.

"But are we merely passing by? Or are we living?
Is time always fleeting? Is there no constant in life?"
I inquired, intrigued.

"The only constant in life is love, and even love is fiddly—
Forever beautiful,
Yet, forever taunting,
Forever reinventing itself," she said.

Regrets

Trapped between
what used to be
and what should have been,
we often neglect what is
and that is our greatest sin

The Silence of Midnight

In the darkest hours
that follow my evening bliss,
the silence of midnight
is my friend and my foe

When all the lights are dimmed,
these dreamless nights
unclog all my senses at once—
And I watch, powerless
as the monsters of my closet
come to life in my mind

Epilogue

The Poet's Mind

Must my stanzas always rhyme?
Must I always abide by orthodox
metrical schemes? Is it not a crime
For emotions to be trapped in a box?

Can't my words
    Just flow freely
        And reflect
           The beautiful
           Chaos
           That is
           Life?

I am...

The bearer of tears
and heartfelt aching,
I am the one
 who hides behind weak similes
to pour his sentiments
on blank pages
and overused canvas

I am a sonnet dragged
by the plea of sorrow,
I am the smile
behind the pain

I am the comforting sheath
of plausible deniability
I am the truth that lies
beneath the lies I have told

I am chastity
to my deflowered Muse,
the ebullience used
to disguise my ruse

I am a poet of fortune
forced to scribble
his languish
in words too weak
to match his aching

I am a usurper
of the third-person,
forced into cowardice
by the vicissitude of life

The Luxury of Sanity

I often fight the urge
to share my poems,
reluctant to be seen
for the wreck that I truly am

But what choice do I have?

I dare not keep
this uncanny mixture
of fear, anger and joy
bottled up inside of me

Poetry is the vessel
without which
I could never afford
the luxury of sanity

From the same author, check out this acclaimed novel **The Illusions of Hope (Hope series, Book 1)**

Coming Soon:

Tears of The Phoenix (Hope Series, Book 2)
I, Erzulie (A historical fiction novel)
Belonging (A poetry collection)

Made in the USA
San Bernardino, CA
14 August 2019